KINGDOM PEARLS (Precious Nuggets for Christian Life)

Apostle Esther P. Joy

Copyright © 2016 Apostle Esther P. Joy

All rights reserved.

ISBN:13: 978- 0692819227
ISBN-10: 0692819223

DEDICATION

Dedicated to the Father and the Son and the Holy Spirit. From whom all blessings flow. Also to my dear husband, my children, spiritual children and spiritual parents. As well as those seeking a closer walk with God.

CONTENTS

	Acknowledgments	i
1	God's way brings His blessing	Pg. #1
2	The Father Knows Best	Pg #4
3	Becoming Like Christ	Pg. #9
4	God Inhabits Our Praise	Pg. #11
5	Prayer Changes Things	Pg. #13
6	Forgiveness Sets You Free	Pg. #19
7	Laziness Brings Poverty	Pg. #23
8	Displaying Christ To others	Pg. #26
9	Train Up Our Children	Pg. #29
10	Rest And Relaxation	Pg. #32

ACKNOWLEDGMENTS

I would like to acknowledge all my teachers and mentors. Those who spoke his will into my life, trained me in righteousness. I can't forget my dear husband , Aaron, who supports and backs up my efforts for God, with his humble service . God bless you .

God's Way Brings Blessings

Blessed is the man that walketh not in the counsel of the ungodly, nor sitteth in the seat of the scornful. But his delight is in the law of the Lord; and in His law doth he meditate day and night. And he shall be like a tree; planted by the rivers of water; that bringeth forth his fruit in his season, his leaf also shall not wither; and whatsoever he doeth shall prosper. (Psalm 1) Your life will thrive and grow when adhering to God's principles. He is the creator, the life-giver and our Heavenly Father. God stated in His Holy word the Bible: "My son keep my commandments and live".(Proverbs 7:2) Every day is a brand new day. A gift from God. We have a fresh and new opportunity to choose who we will serve. We face a decision to serve the Lord our God, or serve the devil. God promises us blessing, joy, eternal life. But the opposite dangles temptation and lies in front of us; in order to deceive, lead astray, and bring forth destruction to the good plans that Father God has for you. It is so important not to associate ourselves with those who would take us to dark situations, wrong choices, wrong places, evil conversations, and away from the blessings of God. Nothing good comes from disobeying God. Just the same as breaking natural laws of the land can bring great consequences, even jail time. So then first of all we need to learn what God's laws are. This is done by reading, studying His word, the Holy Bible. Join a Bible-based, Holy Spirit filled church, or take bible studies with someone knowledgeable in God's word. I don't know about you, but it would be well worth the time to learn something that could save or give me life. God's word is spirit and life; He left it as a guideline for us to follow. Getting to know Him is the most important thing in your entire life. You may think how could it be fun obeying God. Well He is an excellent God. He made us to live, work, create, explore, enjoy, prosper. But because He is wise, all-knowing, He knows what the outcome of destructive behavior would be. If you kill, steal, or destroy, you could end up in jail or dead. If You go around sleeping with everyone you please, you become soul-tied to someone who could be damaging to your soul. Connecting you to someone whom you may want to depart from permanently one day. Doing as we please has effects; drinking too much brings liver damage, smoking cigarettes brings possible cancer. There are results to life's choices. But God is a good God, He wants what is good for us. Jesus said in the book of (3 John 2) "Beloved I wish above all things that thou mayest prosper and be in health, even as thy soul prospers". We need to stay in perimeters of His plans, His laws. Blessed is the man who sitteth not in the counsel of the wicked". Why not surround yourself with Godly people, Godly music, Good environments, peaceful habitations, joyfulness, good reports, good healthy habits, laughter, things that bring life, and a good result. We want to be like a tree; planted by the rivers of water; that bring forth our fruit in our season, so our leaf (life) shall not wither; and whatsoever we do shall prosper. God's ways bring forth Blessings!

The Father Knows Best

The Father knows best! This could be and indeed is the most true statement there is. The Heavenly Father created it all! He knew what we would do before we knew ourselves. He made us with a divine plan in mind. He says in His Holy word,(Jeremiah 1:5) "Before I formed thee in the belly I knew thee; and before thou came forth out of the womb I sanctified thee". God is the only source of truth about our purpose and destiny. The enemy of your soul (the devil) has his own evil plans to thwart you and throw you off course by seducing you to believe in other things and following the wrong people, who lead you in the opposite direction, far from God! This is the beginning of a very destructive downward spiral. The enemy of your soul hates that God loves you so much. He will do anything, absolutely, anything, to stop you from pleasing God. He has made it his solemn goal to steal souls from God. God who created you, wants a one on one relationship with you. He longs to fellowship with you. God wants you to blossom and flourish like a tree by the water. He wants the best for your life. This is why it is so important to get to know Him. He is our Heavenly Father, our God, and our friend. The first thing we must do is repent for all our sins and the way we have lived our lives. Confess the Lord Jesus with our mouth. Repeat this prayer after me when you are ready.

"Lord Jesus, come into my life, come into my heart. Forgive me for all of my sins and the way I have lived my life. I believe that you were born of a virgin, and that you lived as a man. I believe that you were crucified, died on the cross, and rose from the dead on the 3rd day, I make you my Lord and savior". If you confessed this you were born gain. You are a New creation by Christ Jesus! You belong to the Kingdom of The Most High God! God will begin to move over your life by His Power! His Spirit will begin to replace any other spirit. This is a process as He will begin shedding the old grave clothes of darkness from off you. There is a transformation process. What you used to like doing will begin to fade away. Your soul will begin to crave His goodness. This is the greatest gift God can give you, the gift of salvation! Wherever the Spirit of the Lord is, there is Liberty! Lining our lives up with His will is the wisest choice we can make. We need to learn of Him and His commandments. Let me encourage you to start having Bible studies with a true Bible teacher. You want to shun false teachers and false religions. You may also start online Bible studies. Then you need to join a true Christian Church. There are so many churches that profess to be true. But be aware! You want a Bible-based, Holy-Spirit filled church ONLY! In your own personal study time, start reading the book of John in the Bible. Then read through the book of Psalms. This is a great place to start. We are very careful of what we allow into our homes. We are very careful of what we allow into our spirit. For instance, movies full of violence, sexual content, witchcraft, dirty language, will pollute our spirit and destroy the atmosphere. How can you expect to progress into the image of your savior Christ, feeding on the devil's food? Bad things bring bad results, good things bring good results. Remember, in order to thrive you must be connected to things of God. You will now have to rethink old friendships. Yes this is critical. Some of the folk we used to run with could hinder the new thing God wants to do for your life. Someone, smoking, drinking, gambling, lying, cussing and fornicating would be damaging to your new mindset. Could be used as a tool of the devil to keep you in a life of sin. Remember, sin separates us from God. God is a Holy God! He loves righteousness. Righteousness (right living) brings bountiful blessings. Great rewards are a direct result of righteousness. The people who knew us before we came the cross, will think you're strange or lost your mind! They remember how you were, and may mock and ridicule your new found faith in Christ. It's absolutely fine to break ties with them, even relatives! You can offer the salvation of the cross to them, but if they don't receive you, you can break the ties and ask God to break the ties. Then pray Jesus send someone to minister to them in ways they can understand. God wants to save souls. Maybe you can't reach your own loved ones, but He has other ways, The Lord of The Harvest who is Jesus Christ, can reach them. But you got to trust Him. Pray this prayer "Lord Jesus, please open the eyes of my lost loved ones, that they may see that you are Lord and the only way to everlasting life! Lord I apply the Blood you shed on Calvary cross over their minds, hearts, will, emotions, to mark them for you to move by your power! Lord I repent for all their sins and renounce the evil way they have lived. Today I place each one of them in your mighty, delivering, hands for their health, healing, soul-salvation, for your Glory! God you must make haste as the enemy is trying to sift them as wheat and take them to hell! In the name of Jesus, MOVE BY YOUR POWER! I praise you in advance for this miracle! You are an awesome God! Hallelujah!" God is more than able! Trust Him! Trusting Him brings blessings. (Jeremiah 17:" Blessed is the man that trusteth in the Lord; and whose hope the Lord is". We can ask God daily for His help, guidance, His protection, and prosperity. He is for us, not against us. He wants your business to prosper, your health to prosper, the work of your hands, your good relationships, marriages, etc. He owns everything, because He created it all! He truly knows best! We gain wisdom from the "all wise God"! There is no lack in Him. Only love, goodness, mercy, rest for our souls. HE is Father The Son, and the Holy Spirit. Almighty in Power!

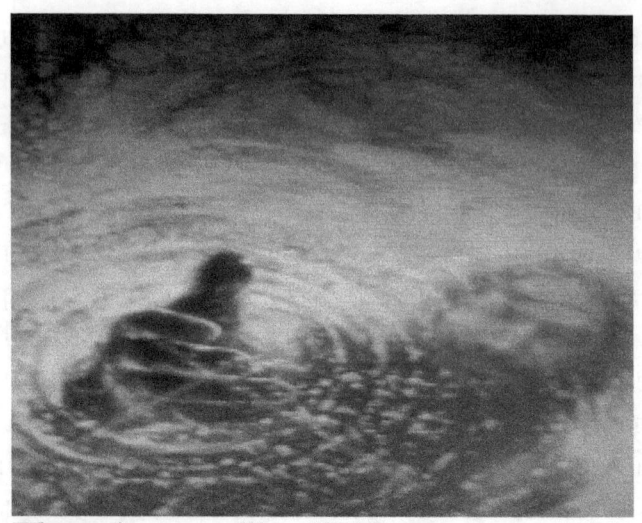

There is none like HIM, no not anywhere! Your faith is all that's required to tap into the greatest relationship of your life! Can you imagine the benefits. Divine health, protection Kingdom blessings. God-given plans versus the plans of the enemy. Direct communication with the Creator, in the name of Jesus Christ. He says I will turn your mess into a message. I will work all things for your good! I am your shield and buckler. Let us go to the other side. Away from all this madness! Yes today, you have chosen to walk into a new door to freedom, restoration, and a new beginning. Don't be afraid and don't look back. The worst is behind, the blessing lies ahead. Forward is the only way! Don't be distracted and don't be snared. Jesus always leads us forward and higher. HE says in His Holy word, "I am the way, the truth and the life"(John 14:6) Nothing is worth missing out on all He has prepared, hold on to His Hand!!!

BECOMING LIKE CHRIST.

When we are saved something miraculous happens to us. We change our thinking and, our desires change. We start seeing what we could not see spiritually before. The Holy Spirit begins a work in our hearts. The Bible tells us that "The Lord is that Spirit, and where the spirit of the Lord is; there is liberty". (1 Cor. 3:17). God wants to begin a work in us to change us into the image of His dear Son, Jesus Christ. God promises to perfect us til the day of Jesus Christ. Remember, it is the grace of God the Father, that we received salvation. This is the greatest gift, through Jesus Christ, one can receive. Spiritual adoption into the Kingdom of God! Assuring us that as we live for God, keeping His laws, heeding His commandments, we will receive eternal life. Remember you are on a journey, like suddenly awakening from a long sleep. You are in spiritual process, transformation from who you once were, to who God created you to be. Your eyes are opening to truth. You are not perfect, but by the sacrifice of the blood of Jesus Christ, you are being perfected. Transformation occurs as you begin to study and meditate on God's Holy word the Bible. Going to the house of the Lord, associating with other believers. Worship brings transformation. You want to surround yourself with those who are like-minded, and shun those who would keep you locked into a dark past. This is a season of progression, not regression. Jesus came to deliver us from evil, from darkness, curses, bondages false religion, and the strongholds of the enemy. It is your responsibility to run after this precious gift like with everything in you! This is your coming out of the grave time. As you get deeper in faith, you will realize a greater peace, sense of freedom, and direction.

Jesus loves you and will walk you all the way out! (Psalms 23:4) " Yea though I walk through the valley of the shadow of death, I will fear no evil for you are with me; thy rod and thy staff they comfort me". Yes he will be with you through the transformation process, from the old you to your new beginning. Just like He was with Daniel in the lion's den, and Joseph in prison. Jesus died on the cross for those who would call upon His name. Start praising Him with your mouth, and from your heart! Rejoice in His love for you that brought you out.

"The Lord is my shepherd; I shall not want; He make me to lie down in green pastures". (ps.23)

God Inhabits The Praises Of His People.

When we praise God from our hearts, we open up heaven. He delights in the sound of our worship with song and words of rejoicing over Him. Praise shows our reverence for His sovereignty and Power. We are humbling ourselves recognizing we cannot live or succeed without His direct help. Praise is one of the most important parts of a true Christian's Life. Praise is such a powerful part of this new relationship with God, that He promises to be wherever He is being praised! Praise says "Thank you Lord". Praise also is a mighty weapon against the forces of darkness. When we take our minds off of trouble and not fall into fear, something mighty happens. Faith is required to please God. Praise says I trust in you Lord! Praise will bring the presence of God. The Bible says that "In His presence is fullness of Joy" (Psalms 16:11). It is a good Idea to fill your house and car with songs of praise and worship. The atmosphere is very important to have peace. The enemy is the "prince of the air". So we need to soak the atmosphere with praise to the Almighty God, His Son, Jesus Christ, and the Holy Spirit. Worship will thwart the enemy's plan, and bring the Kingdom of God! Become a true praise and worshiper from your heart! God knows what is in our Hearts. It must be pure, true, and worthy. It would also be a great thing to try a few Bible believing, Holy Spirit filled churches, til you are comfortable with the right one. Look for one that causes praise and worship. You would be surprised at the number of churches that don't praise and worship God. They have music that is not from God and does not move one to worship. Be very concerned about the music being sung or played! True praise and worship music brings the presence of the Holy Spirit. Without the presence and power of the Holy Spirit, there will be no miracles, healings, deliverances, etc. We need His presence! There is no other greater power than God the Holy Spirit! Be sure to be a part of a group that praises and worships God. It really does not have to be the biggest church in the world. Jesus promised that "Where two or three are gathered in my name, there are I Am in the midst of them". (Matthew 18:20) Praising God is a mandatory act required of the Father! Psalms 150 tells us "Let everything that hath breath praise ye the Lord"! So lift your hands toward the ceiling or sky, and with thanksgiving from your heart; begin to glorify the Father, Jesus, and the Holy Spirit. You can start with "Lord I give you praise, I bless your Holy name, you alone are worthy of all the praise, glory and the Honor!" Lord I worship your sovereignty, your righteousness and your Great Power"! I love you with all my heart, I adore you! Glory to the Father and to the Son and the Holy Spirit ,now and evermore"!!! Let your voice be a carrier of Praise to God! You will enter into His gates and change your life and circumstances in a miraculous way.

PRAYER CHANGES THINGS.

The most important tool in your Christian walk is prayer. Prayer allows you access to the Father. Prayer connects us with the Kingdom allowing us to petition God for His help ,intervention, Power and guidance. We need God's help with every area of our life. He is the source of life and has the answer to any problem, incidence, sickness, etc. God loves it when we depend on Him for all our needs. We approach Him in the name of His Son, our Lord Jesus Christ. We should adopt a powerful prayer life. Every 24 hours is an new day, and we should start it off with prayer of thanksgiving to God for another day of life, for protection for ourselves and loved ones, and who or what you would like to cover. Adopting a good and solid prayer life will ground you in the things of God ,it will also place you in a place of trusting and leaning on Father God for everything ,realizing that we are in need of Him for all and every detail of life. Prayer will draw us close to God, our Jesus Christ, and the Holy Spirit. We have to make it through 24 hours a day. One never knows what the enemy's plans are, but a good prayer life will thwart and derail the enemy's plans. Every morning is a new grace, and it needs to be covered with God's intervention ,guidance, and protection!

POWER of PRAYER

A PRAYER TO START A NEW DAY

" Dear gracious, loving, Heavenly Father, thank you for another day of life. Thank you for choosing me to live. I am sorry for any sins I have not repented for. Please have mercy on me ,and cleanse me of all unrighteousness. Father God I pray for myself and on behalf of my spouse, children, church, ministry affiliates, and my loved ones. Lord God look down upon us this day with your eyes of favor, to guide, and protect us from any hurt, danger or harm. I bind up and break every curse operating against us in any way, shape or form. In the mighty name of Jesus Christ. I loose away sickness, disease, car wrecks, accidents, danger, harm, severe or minor, bodily afflictions, In the holy name of Jesus Christ. I cover us with the whole armor of God, soaked with the Blood of Jesus Christ of Nazareth. I pray your reinforcement angels will surround us as we come and go, in our homes, businesses, workplaces, schools, and all we have to do in our day. Lord lead us in your righteousness ,away from trouble. Fill us with your Holy Spirit and use us for your glory. Thank you for your ever constant presence. I love you and bless your Holy name, thank you God. In the mighty name of Jesus Christ ,my Lord, Amen". You will grow in words, adding more names, places, situations, circumstances. Soon you will just awaken each morning, talking to God in prayer.

Prayer Is Communication With God.

As you become more and more comfortable in speaking with God, your prayer life will expand. You will be more at ease, and even feel confident in interceding to God on other's behalf. Good intercessor's are a gift from God. We need the help of a good prayer warrior. Remembering that this world is unpredictable, we must never take for granted not one second! Keep God involved in your life and day to day affairs. Where the Spirit of the Lord is, there is liberty, goodness, joy, peace, healing, and just everything good. Your prayers must be from your heart. Heartfelt, sincere, prayers, move and touch the hand of God. Remember, we don't need a set of beads or some so-called, "lucky" object. simply approach God with praise and thanksgiving, and We begin to repent for anything not righteous where we could of failed, or repent for anyone we are praying for. All in the name Of Jesus Christ. Then ask him what you need. If you have a prayer partner you can trust, you can touch and agree with them as you pray together. God created us to fellowship with Him. The only way to get our prayers heard is through Jesus Christ. (John 14:6) Jesus told us "I am the way; the truth ,and the life, nobody comes to the Father; except by me". This is the only way God will hear us, it is through the precious name of Jesus". Jesus prayed to the Father when he was here on the earth. We have that same privilege because of what he did for us on the cross, sacrificing his life for us to live.

THE LORD'S PRAYER. Jesus told his disciples "Pray even like this:" Our Father which art in the heaven, hallowed be thy name, thy kingdom come, thy will be done on earth as it is in heaven. Give us this day our daily bread, and forgive us our debts, as we forgive our debtors. Lead us not into temptation, but deliver us from evil. For thine is the kingdom and the power and the glory forever and ever, even forever more. In the name of Jesus Christ, Amen, Amen". (Matthew6:9-13) Your prayers will become more intense and detailed the more you pray to Father. You will even be effective as an intercessor. Someone close or far will always need prayer. Let this amazing gift become your normal daily experience. Talking to God is the utmost, and He is a "very present help in times of trouble". (Psalms 46:1).

FORGIVENESS

Hatred, anger and bitterness are very evil emotions. These emotions will eat the soul and destroy the one who houses them. I knew a man that hated a woman so much til he was obsessed with revenge. All he could think about, waking and going to bed, was destroying her life. The woman went on to serve the Lord. She learned forgiveness, but he was poisoned with hatred. His whole body was literally rotting. Neglecting his own health and hygiene, he decayed and stank really bad. Consumed with destroying this one particular woman was eating this man alive. You will be bound and unable to move forward when filled with unforgiveness. In most cases the other person moves on while you are stuck in a period of time and on a set of past events and circumstances. Wrong emotions are part of the soul. These are very strong influences that cloud judgement, impair rational thinking.

In order to progress, we must let go of all hatred, anger, and bitterness.

Jesus Christ died on the cross to offer us a new life With him and the Heavenly Father. His blood sacrifice has given all who repent of their sins and confess him as Lord, a chance at a whole new life. As only God can give. But unforgiveness cancels this grand new opportunity at life. It is completely against all Jesus stands for. He is willing to forgive us for our sins but we must forgive others. The Lord is not blind nor naïve to your enemy's devices. He sits up high and looks down low, and knows any evil that has been done to you. He also knows the hurt involved from, rejection, molestation, angry words, or whatever hurt you. But he offers you relief from bondages of darkness such as hatred, that will destroy your soul. You cannot go forward and be blessed as long as you hate. You will sit life on the sidelines and watch everyone else live, work, thrive, come and go. Hatred will bind up your life and tie you to the person emotionally, Binding you to the past . There is nothing worse than being so intent on getting a person back for long ago hurts, til you sabotage your own self! Allowing them to control your mind, and emotions every single waking day. This is just what the enemy, the devil, wants to happen. So he can kill two birds with one stone. Destroying people's lives is his agenda. But remember, The Father in heaven wants you free. Free to work, love, prepare, go forward, mostly to serve Him. Let this be a new day to "forgive".

PRAYER TO FORGIVE

"Lord Jesus come into my life, come into my heart, forgive me for all my sins and help me to forgive all those who have hurt me. Lord I've been abused, hurt and rejected by _____ and I'm finding it so hard to forgive. Please heal me and my soul of negative emotions. Lord take evil from me. Give me a new and right spirit. Help me to get over this and past this hurt so I can live a full life that pleases you. Lord I thank you for hearing this prayer and saving me". In your name Jesus, amen.   You must choose to forgive, forgiveness is a choice. Jesus knows somethings just hurt us so bad, but he offers a way out. Your blessings are tied up in forgiveness. Forgiving others frees the soul and breaks the chains of torment, hatred, vengeance and destruction. For as long as you hold another hostage to how they hurt you, is as long as you stand still; unable to grow, move on and be healthy and happy. Obsession with hurt, anger and revenge, will destroy.

FORGIVE AND BE SET FREE.

(Mark 11:25) " And when you stand praying, forgive, if ye have ought against any; that your Father also which is in Heaven may forgive you your trespasses".

LAZINESS BRINGS POVERTY

Lazy people waste precious time. Your time is priceless. Once a moment passes by, it is gone forever. God has designed mankind to be productive, fruitful. He made us to work and accomplish. Work brings reward. But idleness bring destruction. Good work is so important to God till He has it written in His word: "If a man would not work; neither should he eat". (Thessalonians 3:10) There is a rich reward in rising each day and going to be productive. Bills need to be paid. Your family cannot survive without finances coming in the home. Even a single person has expenses and needs an income. God gave each of us talents, gifts, and, abilities. When we put in honest work we earn wages or when we do legal

business, we profit. There is a special gift inside you. Maybe you love drawing, sewing, or singing. Maybe you love designing or computers. Some have gift of gab and will do well in sales, preaching, lecturing. You are unique in yourself. No one is like you. However, some waste time sitting around, with no ambition, goals, or desire to achieve.
When we sit around day to day, doing nothing, we live wasted life with nothing to show for it. Laziness bring poverty, and destitute ,embarrassing ,shame! What a pity to stand before Father God one day and did not do anything with the precious life and gifts He has given you. Have you become discouraged by not succeeding ? Maybe failed at something, or suffered word curses from an authority figure telling you ,"you will never amount to anything"? Whatever your situation, it is time to get back up again, dusting yourself off, and believe what God says about you. Don't share your goals with anyone except those who celebrate you. God wants you to work, achieve, and prosper. Jesus said in (3rd John) "Beloved, I wish above things that you would prosper and be in health, even as thy soul prospers. Maybe you are great with the garden, you would be a blessing to others as a landscaper. You could go to the county clerk and start your very own landscaping company, with just a lawnmower,

shovel and a few tools. Some are cut out for the 9-5 schedule. Some bake good cakes and desserts. Others are good at cleaning, typing, nursing. When you get up and get out, to share your gift or skill, or talent, you contribute to the community and society. Also your household prospers and not lacks, nor wants for anything. You become a productive citizen and most certainly a blessing to your family, church, and to God. God wants you to win to produce, to have victory. We should never take ourselves and our contribution for granted. Someone is in need of us. A productive day brings a sense of accomplishment, a sense of worth. Here are some Bible scriptures against laziness.

1.)Proverbs 20:13 "Love not sleep lest thou come to poverty; open thy eyes and thou shall be satisfied with bread".
2.)Proverbs 10:4 "He becometh poor that dealeth with a slack hand; but the hand of the diligent maketh rich".

Displaying Christ To Others

When we become saved, born again, and have the privilege of a relationship with God, we also have a great responsibility to bear witness to others who may not know of Him. When going about our daily affairs, working, at school, doing business, or just doing things in our own neighborhood. People see you. They hear what you say, see what you do. They only know you by the works you do or how you look, appear, and or carry yourself. We must realize that most times our only witness of Jesus to someone through ourselves is how we appear to them. How we dress ourselves, wear our hair, or even if we comb our hair at all. Or speech, what we say, even our attitude. If I'm cussing and yelling at the least opportunity because things don't go my way ,or I feel some kind of way, I'm not displaying Christ at all. Is the property cared for, is there junk all over the porch or backyard? How would others perceive you? How do you appear in public? What would your neighbors or a stranger or co-worker say to describe you? Would someone give you a good reference? How would the Lord Himself describe you. We represent Jesus to others with our looks, actions, appearances, and how we live and treat others. God sees our every move. No one is perfect, but it must be our goal each day to live for God. Dressed neatly, clean hygeine, home clean, outside the home clean and neat. Even those who know you can say there is something so special about you, and you are pleasant to be around. This is called "impressions". It's amazing to see people in a public store like Walmart, cussing, smelling bad, wearing dirty clothes. This does not fit the image of a blessed Lord and King. How we carry ourselves can go a long way I our walk with God and in leading others to God. Would you be quick to follow someone drunk? Would you be quick to follow someone cussing and smelly? God expects us to clean up our lives not just spiritually ,but also physically. It is our witness that we have been changed from the inside out. I think about my early days as an evangelist meeting people on the street, taking food to the people's home. You would be surprised at what you see in and around their homes. My God! How anyone can live among rubbish, trash, old food wrappers and bugs! People who go to church, professing they are saved. Houses looking like they worship the devil. Filthiness is a demonic spirit. "Spirit of Filth"! That is not how we are to display ourselves. God is beautiful, light, perfect, Holy! You do not have to be rich to be clean. Simply clean, and organize what you do have. Throw out clutter, wash dishes daily, take out the trash, etc. Tend to your personal hygeine daily, and before bed. Practice good clean habits til you are used to living a clean life. Be aware of cleanliness. Watch how you communicate to others. Use good speech. The Bible tells us "Let no corrupt communication proceed out of your mouth; but that which is good to the use of edifying, that it may minister grace to the hearer". (Ephesians 4:29) We got to be very careful. Someone is always watching just to see if you really are who you say you are in Christ. Women dress ladylike, not whorish, and seducing, but beautiful and elegant. It is just a good idea to practice cleanliness and decency. God is clean and Holy. We have a great privilege to live for Him through the shed blood of His precious son. No greater sacrifice can ever be made! God can take bad cleaning and hygeine habits from you. Repent and ask for His help. You are on your way to a life that represents Christ . I've always been clean and organized from a child. I just loved to see each room clean, beds made, dishes washed, etc. But it wasn't true with some of those around me back then. Some of us just need to adopt these habits that weren't naturally embedded in us. This is so important to how others perceive you. Especially when seeking employment, promotions, doing business, church, etc. God is watching and sees how we live this life He gave us. What is so good about it, is that you can seek God's help and ask Him to help you. I love the book of Psalms 51"create in me a clean heart, renew in me a new and right spirit". God can give us a spirit of cleanliness. If this is your prayer, just ask Him.

Train Up Your Child

We as Christians also have responsibility to raise our children in the Lord. Our way of life before them should be a godly example of how they should also live their lives. Right from home is where they will learn from example. If you are living any kind of way ,then they will pick up that this is okay. If you stay out all night and come home drunk, they will tend to think this is normal. Children are easy to impress. Ungodly parents usually ruin what plans God has for their life. They love their parents and believe in them no matter what they do. God trusts us to raise them up to be productive citizens, but mostly God-fearing individuals. How they are reared means everything. Their minds are impressionable. Their mommy and daddy cussing and lying, they think it's okay to cuss and lie. If they see you stealing and robbing, they grow up believing it is okay to rob and steal from others. I've seen many cases of parents leading their kids to hell. Usually they will take up their parents religious beliefs. This is really where you want to be ever so attentive. Whatever your "religion" will most likely be their "religion". The truth is that God who created the heavens and the earth, is not religious. He is The Almighty God! His the Father, the Son, and the Holy Spirit. He has a

Kingdom. He would never divide himself into this and that! God wants us to worship Him, praise Him, Bless and adore Him, and Fear Him! All in the name of Jesus Christ. Jesus is the only way, the truth and the life! (John 14:6) You see you don't need manmade religious doctrines. You need a solid relationship with God. You need to read the Bible with your children and learn of God's laws and commandments and what He requires of our Christian life. Find a good Bible-believing, Holy Spirit filled church to attend for guidance, fellowship, and support. Remember you are responsible for how you shape your children's spirituality. When in doubt I always direct others to Genesis 1:1 "In the beginning "God" created the heavens and the earth". This was an introduction to who the true and living God is. Teach your children to worship this God! Teach them to pray to Him in the name of Jesus Christ. Always remember your children look up to you as mentor ,role model, and God does too! You will be a major factor in how they form and grow as adults. Lead them to a life with Christ Jesus as their savior. Teach them godly truths, and the Bible. Watch what comes across the tv or what they read ,see or do. You want Gods hand upon them. Dedicate them to heavenly Father. Give them back to Him, anoint them with oil, and bless them. Declare they will be god-fearing and successful. Train them up in the way that they should go. They are your inheritance, a gift. You are all they have and the most influence they will know. Their hearts and belief will center around what "mommy or daddy used to do.

Rest And Relaxation

In order to thrive and accomplish day to day activities, chores, work schedule, even worship, there must be a balance. We are human beings. God made us to live ,work, play, then rest. In order to be effective in our family life, ministry, business, or job, there must be a rest period. Some people work 12 and 16 hours a day and wonder why their home life suffers, their relationships suffer, and mostly their health suffers. This is not to tell you to not be diligent, but to find balance. You can only do so much before the body becomes overloaded. You can work a horse too much, even they will give out. By realizing that God gave us a heart that beats, and we must take care of it and not overload it by working, worrying, or anything in excess. Our system becomes overloaded by taxing ourselves too much. Whether you are a Pastor, nurse, janitor, housekeeper, homemaker, etc., You must know when to rest! This is one life lesson that must be heeded. I know some prayer warriors who are overtaxing themselves. Remember we are not God, God is God. There is a time to fight a battle ,with God's help, and then there is a time to rest in God. Knowing the battle belongs to Him. We need at least 6-8hrs sleep a night. Some work schedules may not allow this, but you must find this rest time somewhere in the course of a 24 hour day, even in power naps. The Bible tells us " God rested on the 7th day" (Genesis 2:3) You have got to set aside time for peace, rest, and time with Heavenly Father. He is the source of life. The Bible says(" He is the husbandman, Jesus is the true vine, we are the branches" John 15:1) We cannot live without the source of life. We stay connected to him by worship or praising, sometimes just listening to a soft praise song and laying before Him. The Spirit of the Lord is saying "rest in me". We sometimes have to get away or just not answer the phone to avoid unnecessary distractions. It really is okay to avoid other people's drama. Protecting your peace is the right thing to do. Without proper rest we overload the system of our bodies and can cause serious damage or consequences. Jesus invited us to come to Him, saying "Come to me you who labor and are heavy laden and I will give you rest". (Matthew 11:28) We need rest, it's okay to rest, our bodies require rest and God has ordained rest as a human requirement. When we rest and just step back from it all, things don't seem so important. You realize it's okay to let that go today. It's okay not to answer the phone today. There will be nothing anyway without our health. God says it's okay, let go and step back a minute.

Prayer of Salvation

If you do not know Jesus Christ as your Lord and savior, repeat this prayer : "Lord Jesus, come into my life, come into my heart, forgive me for my sins and the way I've lived my life. I believe you died on the cross and you rose from the dead on the third day and ascended to heaven to sit at the right side of the Father, I make you my Lord and savior". Congratulations and welcome into the Kingdom Of God!

ABOUT THE AUTHOR

She is President ,Founder, Visionary,of "Kingdom Power Ministries Intl. Inc.",Senior Pastor of "Kingdom Power Ministries Intl. Church" in Clinton Township, Michigan. She is a televangelist and producer of "A Beautiful Life Now", seen Mondays 5 pm est, on The Now Network, www.thenownetwork.org, Or Roku, Other stations. www.kingdompowerministriesintl.com Available for bookings contact : totallyrestore@yahoo.com

Apostle Esther Joy is a humble servant of the Lord God. A wife. She is gifted in many talents. God graced her with a voice to sing, songwriting, author, she is an artist, fashion designer, interior designer, business woman, televangelist, life coach, mother, wife.

www.ingramcontent.com/pod-product-compliance
Lightning Source LLC
LaVergne TN
LVHW051205080426
835508LV00021B/2826